DEAR BOBBY

Praise for *Dear Bobby*

"There is so much we don't know as a collective when it comes to energy and the soul, and what happens after death. What I do know from the depths of my own heart, is that the soul knows where home is, and love is the vehicle that leads us there. Spanning lifetime after lifetime. The soul, like love, lives on, even after death. It's us humans who suffer through this heartbreaking journey. Diane Zappa's first book, *The Married Widow*, cemented the belief that the soul knows the way home.

Now, with her second book, *Dear Bobby: My Grief Journey*, proves once again that true, unconditional love remains. That even death cannot extinguish a love that was written in the stars."

—Jennifer Seitzer

"If you are struggling with deep loss, you will find many handholds here. Diane is a writer who carries you along as easily as a summer wave. Her flowing narrative is a soft place to land, providing understanding along with help in coping with devastating loss. Diane's background in research guided her to accumulate many resources to deal with her own terrible loss when her dear husband suddenly collapsed, never to awaken. She shares all of them generously, including some very touching, intimate, and heartwarming letters to her departed husband that she continues to write. For her, writing is solace: it is both connection and therapy. She encourages you to try, furnishing quotes to prompt your thoughts, and wise advice not to worry about grammar or spelling. As well, you'll find books to read and online groups to join. It's a book you can pick and choose, not read cover to cover, but one to reach for when you need guideposts or understanding. She makes a very hard time just a little easier."

—Jane Moody, retired therapist

"Diane Papalia Zappa has deepened our awareness of grieving a loved one's passing while entering into the infinite, yet navigable, realm of being a widow. Separated by death, yet paradoxically joined for life via innumerable loving memories of everyday living, even newer bonds of affection are forged—so intimately personal, yet so universally welcoming and human. Here is a magnificent portal into the voices of the heart: each chapter enlightens, enriches, and empowers. The 'Dear Bobby' letters are precious.

This is a compendium of wisdom, including guidelines for writing and living through one's own grief. This is a must acquisition and a compelling read."

—Ephraim Frankel, PhD, LMFT

"Diane has done it again and touched our hearts with her amazing story about her life with Bobby. It is a must read for anyone who has loved and in particular for those of us who have loved and lost. It was a love that was 'meant to be' and nothing could stop it, even over the years. Diane and Bobby had more in the time that they were together than others have had in many more years. They were truly like one person. Thank you, Diane, for making me both smile and cry."

—Lana Rudner

"For anyone who is grieving the loss of a spouse, *Dear Bobby: My Grief Journey* is a comforting read that includes a multitude of valuable resources for support. Like spending time with a trusted friend, Diane's 'Dear Bobby' letters help to lessen the agonizing feeling that we are alone in our grief."

—Vera Armstrong

"Diane's deep understanding of psychology as well as the trauma of her devastating loss make her uniquely qualified to offer this book to those of us who are struggling with grief. The 'Dear Bobby' section brought me to tears!"

—Leela Pratt, executive director,
Young Performers International

"Diane's book brings tears to my eyes. Her love of her late husband was so pure and deep. And now she is using her grieving experience to help others cope with loss by sharing her experience and excellent tips. A fitting tribute to her beloved."

—Maria Leonard Olsen, attorney, podcaster, and author of *50 After 50: Reframing the Next Chapter of Your Life*

"*Dear Bobby: My Grief Journey* is not merely a book which discusses widowhood and offers coping mechanisms to help deal with it. *Dear Bobby* is an incredible lifeline of hope, especially for those of us who were rudely thrust into widowhood with absolutely no warning other than knowing everybody dies. What I thought was insane I discovered was perfectly normal after reading this book. Coping strategies became reality to me. I cannot thank you enough for the clarity this book offers."

—Marion Hook

"Diane Zappa had already written a powerful love story for the ages with *The Married Widow*, a book that proves that true love can survive anything that comes to claim it, including the tragic death of her husband Bob (brother of composer Frank) shortly after they finally exchanged wedding vows, the culmination of a love that remained true for decades, despite distance, and other obstacles.

In her new book, *Dear Bobby: My Grief Journey*, Diane offers a light for a dark place. How does one nourish a grieving soul? Is there a way to continue to stand strong and honor that love after your loved one has departed? There is hope, and this book is a powerful reminder that, even in the most desperate of circumstances, one is not alone.

Simply put, this is another work of true beauty from a brilliant writer."

—Scott Parker, host, *Zappacast*, the official Frank Zappa podcast

"*Dear Bobby: My Grief Journey* is a touching real life love story of the author, Diane Papalia Zappa, and her husband, Bob Zappa, brother of musician Frank Zappa. It is a perfect follow up to Diane's previous book, *The Married Widow*.

As a recent widow, I found Diane's letters to Bobby sweet, intimate, and a wonderful way of dealing with the grief of a lost love. Her book is also very helpful with references to publications, movies, support groups, and Facebook groups that will help widows to deal with their losses. Their story is timeless—a couple experiencing deep, ecstatic love, and later the widow experiencing excruciating loss. It is the tale of a sad and sudden death and the ensuing sorrow, yet it is happy and optimistic in its outlook, as illustrated by the very gracious way Diane has handled her grief.

This is a must read for anyone who has lost a loved one."

—Janet Binder Houts, JD

"I have the unique and treasured perspective of having known Diane Papalia Zappa from the moment she met her beloved Bob until he left her side.

How wonderful to have this absolutely touching companion piece to *The Married Widow: My Journey with Bob Zappa*. You are sure to enjoy her friendly writing style as she addresses her most personal feelings around her love and her loss. In *Dear Bobby: My Grief Journey*, we are reminded that even after death there remains a strong living connection with those we have so strongly loved. This is a book to refer to as we each experience our own losses.

Diane and Bob's true life romance was a beautiful and magical journey to witness."

—Susan M. Nichols, M.S.

DEAR BOBBY

MY GRIEF JOURNEY

DIANE PAPALIA ZAPPA

Albrodo Publishing
New York, NY

Albrodo Publishing, New York, NY
dianepapaliazappa.com

This book is a memoir and it reflects the author's present
recollections of experiences over time.

First edition: September 2023

Library of Congress Control Number: 2023916091

ISBN: 979-8-9889814-0-4 (paperback)
ISBN: 979-8-9889814-1-1 (e-book)

Text and cover design by Sue Balcer
Author photo by Maggie Yurachek Photography

Printed in the United States of America
10 9 8 7 6 5 4 3 2 1

Dear Bobby,

You'll always be the one.
This book is for you.

Love,

Diane

CONTENTS

PART ONE

OUR STORY

CHAPTER ONE

FALLING IN LOVE

When I saw you I fell in love. And you smiled because you knew.

—**Arrigo Balto**

My husband, Charles Robert (Bob) Zappa, passed away suddenly and unexpectedly on December 8, 2018. We had been married for just over three years. He was seventy-five when he died; I was seventy-one when I became a widow.

This is our love story.

***

I met Bob Zappa in 1986 when I was professor of child and family studies at the University of Wisconsin-Madison. I had been invited to a McGraw Hill sales meeting in Princeton, New Jersey that January to celebrate the success of my textbook, *Psychology* by Diane E. Papalia and Sally W. Olds. The text sold over 50,000 copies the year it came out, a virtually unheard of achievement in the world of college publishing. It was named the McGraw Hill Book of the Year 1985 and Bob, the marketing manager for our textbook, was named marketing manager of the year.

Bob and I spent quite a lot of time together at that sales meeting, especially during the hour-long car ride from the Newark airport where he picked me up to drive me to Princeton, and enjoyed each other's company at two dinners. Reminiscing about it later, we both recalled an intense and immediate connection. Looking back, we realized that was when we fell in love.

Through the years, we stayed in touch periodically, mostly by mail, email, and phone, but lost contact in 2006. Then, in August 2013, Bob sent me a letter and told me his wife had passed away earlier that year and that he hadn't forgotten me. It had been seven years since I had heard from him! I had been divorced since 1999, so we were both free to see each other and explore those early feelings.

We decided to meet in October 2013. He came up from his home in New Jersey and we spent the weekend together at my place in Manhattan, and all the old feelings of love and connection came flooding back. The second time we got together—just two weeks later—he got down on one knee and proposed. Of course, I said yes as he placed a diamond engagement ring on my trembling hand.

Our wedding was a lavish affair held at the Hôtel Plaza Athénée in New York City on Saturday, September 26, 2015. The weather was perfect, a crisp autumn day, and the setting was beautiful, with its distinctly French flair. Guests flew in from all over, some from as far away as Belgium and Sweden. The ceremony, accompanied by The Chamberlain Brass quintet, was brief, lasting only about ten minutes. The reception included a cocktail hour and a four-course sit-down dinner with an open bar for seventy people in the hotel's elegant dining room, Arabelle. The day before the wedding, and the day after, we had smaller, more intimate receptions in our suite for family and friends from out of town. Tuxedo-clad butlers served a selection of hors d'oeuvres to the twenty guests at each event.

After four days of celebrating, we easily settled into a very happy married life. Bob loved to go out and explore his new city, often walking in Central Park a few blocks from our home or exercising at a nearby gym. He was especially amused when tourists would ask *him* for directions. They often wanted to know where the memorial to John Lennon, Strawberry Fields, was located in Central Park. And he was happy to tell them. Bob enjoyed our duplex apartment in a prewar condominium called The Level Club on Manhattan's Upper West Side. He readily took to city life. And when we were together—which was most of the time—we spent a lot of time talking and laughing, thrilled that we were finally married.

Early in 2016, however, Bob developed troubling symptoms. He had difficulty picking up objects like utensils, pens, and coins. He said he felt like he was always wearing boxing gloves. Eventually, he could no longer drive or write. His feet became so swollen that he needed help putting on his shoes. He told me he felt like he was walking on bubble wrap. His balance was so compromised that by 2017 he had to use a walker. He also needed special built-up utensils that he could grasp in order to eat.

He tried hand therapy, acupuncture, and massage therapy for his problems, but they didn't relieve his symptoms. He had surgery for carpal tunnel syndrome, which did not improve his condition. He went to several specialists and, finally, after two years of misdiagnosis (and inappropriate treatment), he was eventually diagnosed with the hereditary form of a rare and often fatal disease, amyloidosis. Amyloidosis occurs when a protein called amyloid builds up in a person's organs and systems. It is often difficult to diagnose. Bob had both cardiac and neurological involvement. We found out later that carpal tunnel syndrome can be an early sign of amyloidosis. Unfortunately, no one connected those dots. Had that connection been made early in his disease, there might have been an earlier diagnosis and a different outcome. It breaks my heart to think about that.

But we felt hopeful when he was invited to participate in a clinical trial at the world-famous Neurological Institute of New York at Columbia University located in upper Manhattan. Every few weeks, beginning in January 2018, he underwent a three-hour infusion of a promising drug. His doctors actually thought he was improving.

Sadly, it was too little, too late. Bob passed away that December after eleven months of treatment.

DIANE AND BOB ON THEIR WEDDING DAY.
(Photo courtesy of Maggie Yuracheck Photography.)

CHAPTER 2

OUR FAMILIES

People destined to meet will do so, apparently by chance, at precisely the right moment.

—Ralph Waldo Emerson

Bob and I came from different worlds, but fate connected us. We grew up on opposite sides of the country and with different socioeconomic backgrounds. Still, we instantly connected with each other and shared many of the same values.

BOB'S FAMILY AND BACKGROUND

Charles Robert (Bob) Zappa was born on August 29, 1943 in Baltimore, Maryland. His parents, Francis and Rose Marie Zappa, both had Italian roots. His family was traditional old school Italian. In his memoir, *Frankie and Bobby: Growing Up Zappa*, Bob described his father as "authoritarian and stubborn" and his mother as "a quiet woman, a good cook, and a wonderful mother." His father made the decisions in the family, and the others had no choice but to comply.

Bob was the second oldest of four siblings: Frank (1940–1993), Bob (1943–2018), Carl (1947–2020), and Patrice (1951–), whom Carl nicknamed Candy because he thought she was sweet!

In 1951, when Bob was eight years old and still living in Maryland, his father, a scientist and mathematician, took a position at the Naval Postgraduate School in Monterey, California.

The Zappa family accompanied him and moved at least seven times within California because Bob's father frequently changed jobs. With each move, Bob had to make new friends and adapt to new schools and new communities. But learning how to deal with and even thrive in these situations were survival skills that served him well later in life.

When Bob was seventeen, his father announced that he had accepted a job in Florida. Although Bob dreaded the prospect of yet another move, he was stunned to learn that his father was leaving him behind in California. By this time, his older brother, Frank, had already moved away from home and embarked on his career as a musician. So, Bob's dad, mom, Carl, and Candy left for Florida, leaving Bob to fend for himself. Fortunately, an older friend reached out and offered Bob a place to live until he graduated from high school in 1961.

Later in life when Bob and I were together, he often talked with me about his feelings of abandonment over this incident. These feelings affected him throughout his adult life.

Since his parents didn't encourage his education, Bob had no solid college plans. He started at California State Polytechnic University in Pomona, California, but dropped out after only three months. Bob next enlisted in the US Marine Corps and endured basic training in San Diego. While in the Marines during the Cuban Missile Crisis of 1962, he participated in the blockade around Cuba and then served a tour of duty in Vietnam. He was honorably discharged in 1964.

The Marines gave Bob a needed sense of structure and belonging to something bigger than himself. He was always proud of being a Marine and would say, "Once a Marine, always a Marine." And he used to love telling me, "Not every girl has her own Marine!"

After serving in the Marines, Bob went back to school. He earned a bachelor's degree in history and political science from California State Polytechnic University in Pomona in 1969, followed in 1970 by a research diploma in sociology from the Stockholm University in Sweden.

In 1964, Bob met Marcia Lesheski, a psychiatric nurse from San Diego. They married four months later in January 1965 and had one child, a son, Stanley Jason, in 1971. Bob's first employment consisted of a series of menial jobs, but with a small child he knew he needed to find a job with more security and benefits. In 1971, he accepted a position as sales representative for McGraw Hill, one of the country's largest and most prestigious publishing companies. Bob excelled as a rep. In 1975, he was offered and subsequently accepted the position of physics editor. He and his family left California and moved to Ridgewood, New Jersey, a bedroom community located just outside of Manhattan where the McGraw Hill corporate headquarters are located. While at McGraw Hill, Bob held several positions including senior marketing manager, the position he held when we first met. Bob left McGraw Hill in 1986.

After leaving McGraw Hill, Bob accepted a position as general manager of Datapro, a subsidiary of McGraw Hill located in Delran, New Jersey, eventually becoming vice president. One major job responsibility was to establish a Datapro branch office in Lausanne, Switzerland. That task required him to often be there for weeks at a time. He told me later that one of his biggest regrets about that period of his life was having to be away from his teenage son so often.

After leaving Datapro in 1988, he moved on to several other managerial positions working for publishing companies such as Macmillan, Prentice Hall, and Simon & Schuster.

But Bob had become weary of corporate life and wanted to make a career change. After some thirty years in publishing, he decided to apply to become a New York City Teaching Fellow through a program designed to recruit teachers to work in understaffed schools in low-income areas of the city. The year Bob applied there were about 16,000 applications. Only about 2,400 were accepted, and only 1,600 completed the program. Bob was one of the 1,600. Through that program, he earned a master's degree in education from Lehman College of the City University of New York (CUNY). So, at the age of fifty-nine, Bob began teaching in a number of high-risk schools in the Bronx. Every so often he'd text me that his school was on lockdown because someone with a weapon had gotten in. Bob excelled and thrived as a teacher. His former principal told me that Bob had "changed lives!" He believed it was his calling. After eleven years of teaching, he retired in 2014 at the age of seventy.

After retiring from teaching, Bob began to write. In 2015, he self-published *Frankie and Bobby: Growing Up Zappa* in which he discussed his relationship with his brother, the iconic composer and musician, Frank Zappa, during their

THE ZAPPA SIBLINGS:
CANDY, FRANK, CARL, AND BOB

shared childhood and young adulthood. Next, he self-published *Frankie and Bobby: The Rest of Our Story*. Both were well received with many positive reviews on Amazon and elsewhere. He also wrote a series of astute political commentaries that had a large following on Facebook. Bob was working on a manuscript about his experiences teaching in the Bronx, but passed away before it could be completed.

DIANE'S FAMILY AND BACKGROUND

I was born on April 26, 1947 in Englewood, New Jersey. My parents, Edward and Madeline Papalia, had Italian roots. They had both been born in New Jersey, but all four of my grandparents were from Italy. My mother's family was from Piedmont in the north, and my father's family was from Rome and Sicily.

Like Bob's family, my family was also traditional. My father was an attorney and my mother was a stay-at-home mom who took care of me and my younger brother, Eddie. Life for me was much more stable than it had been for Bob. When I was four years old, my family moved into the house my parents had designed and built in the Palisade section of Fort Lee, New Jersey. It was a beautiful home in a beautiful area. We could see the sparkling lights of New York City and the cars on the George Washington Bridge from the living room. It was my favorite view! I lived there until I went away to college in 1964. And my parents remained there until they had passed; my father in 1992 and my mother in 1999.

Like Bob, I was raised Catholic. For ten years, I attended Academy of the Holy Angels, a

Catholic school that was then located in Fort Lee, New Jersey. And like Bob, I abandoned the Catholic faith in my teen years. In 1962, I transferred to the Dwight School for Girls (now known as the Dwight-Englewood School) in Englewood, New Jersey. It was academically rigorous and I thrived there. I especially loved that we were encouraged to challenge ourselves intellectually, to think outside the box. We were even urged to read the banned books that had been forbidden by my Catholic school!

After I graduated from Dwight, I went to Vassar College in Poughkeepsie, New York. At that time, it was an all-girls school. Perhaps because I was one of the youngest in my class and had never been away from home on my own, I struggled academically. I was simply unprepared for the level of rigor Vassar demanded. But I persisted and graduated on schedule in 1968 with a major in psychology and a minor in French. I still remain friends with a number of women I met there.

Next, I enrolled in a graduate program in child development at West Virginia University in Morgantown, and was awarded an MS degree in Child Development and Family Relations in 1970. While there, I was mentored by a professor, Frank H. Hooper, who encouraged me to pursue the PhD degree. In 1971, I received my doctorate in Lifespan Developmental Psychology. I was 24. I loved graduate school and was fortunate to participate in one of the first programs in the country to study the entire lifespan, not just child and adolescent development. The thinking back then was that nothing "interesting" happened psychologically during the later years. But programs such as this one helped demolish that notion.

Following WVU, I landed a tenure track position at the University of Wisconsin-Madison, one of the most prestigious research institutions in the country. One of my main responsibilities was to teach a course in child and adolescent development and to design a follow-up course covering development through late adulthood. These were undergraduate lecture courses that typically enrolled six hundred or so students each semester. Because of these huge enrollments, I was often approached by publishers' representatives wanting me to consider adopting one (or more) of their textbooks.

But one day, the McGraw Hill rep dropped by my office to tell me that they were looking for a "fresh new voice" to write a textbook on child and adolescent development. He thought that since I was already teaching such a course, I'd be the ideal candidate and asked if he could submit my credentials to the publisher for consideration. Even though it was unusual for an assistant professor to write a textbook, particularly at an institution like UW-Madison with its strong research orientation, I was intrigued.

In 1972, the day after Nixon was re-elected President, Rob Fry, an editor from McGraw Hill's corporate offices in New York, flew out to Madison for our first meeting. A few months later, I signed a contract to write *A Child's World: Infancy through Adolescence* with Sally W. Olds, a professional writer. That book rapidly became *the* market leader, selling over 100,000 copies in its first edition. It is currently in its thirteenth edition. I was then asked to write a text covering the entire lifespan, so Sally Olds and I coauthored *Human Development*. That, too, became a market leader. The fifteenth edition was published in January 2023.

While at the UW-Madison, I also taught graduate level human development courses, usually focused on adulthood and aging; conducted research on cognitive functioning in late life; and had articles published in refereed professional journals. I was promoted to associate professor with tenure in 1975 and two years later, at age thirty, I attained the rank of full professor of child and family studies.

In June 1976, I married Jonathan Finlay, a British doctor who had studied medicine at the University of Birmingham in England. Shortly before we married, he moved to Wisconsin where he held several fellowships in the pediatrics department at UW. In 1980, he was offered a position at Stanford's Lucile Packard Children's Hospital in Palo Alto, California. Since I was able to take a two-year leave from my position in Madison, we moved west. While there, Sally Olds and I began writing our introductory text, *Psychology*. Once my two-year leave was up, we moved back to Madison where Jonathan accepted a position as Assistant Professor of Pediatrics. We also adopted an eight-week-old baby girl, Anna Victoria, who was born in Chile in 1986.

In 1987, Jonathan was offered a position at Children's Hospital of Pennsylvania (known as CHOP) so I resigned from my professorship at UW-Madison and we moved east where I spent my time revising my textbooks and taking care of Anna. Then, in 1989, he accepted the position of Vice Chairman of Pediatrics at Memorial Sloan Kettering Cancer Center (MSKCC) in New York City. I loved the idea of moving to Manhattan as it was just a few miles from my parents, and I could be near them during the last years of their lives. I found the city vibrant and I was thrilled to be living there. And I was delighted to be able to continue my career as a textbook author while working from home.

Sadly, our marriage didn't last, and we divorced in 1999. I'm fortunate that I still see Anna often. And when Bob was alive, the three of us spent many fun and stimulating evenings with her discussing everything from work, to politics, to dreams of travel. The two of them had formed a close bond. Anna is thirty-seven now, works in Manhattan, and lives just over a mile away from me. It's comforting to know that she is nearby, especially now that I'm alone.

When Bob and I talked about our different backgrounds, I would tease, "Besides being Italian, what do we have in common?" And he would reply, "We are one person." I believe that to be true.

DIANE AND HER BROTHER, ED.
(Photo courtesy of
Maggie Yurachek Photography.)

CHAPTER 3

OUR LAST NIGHT

When he shall die, Take him and cut him out in little stars, And he will make the face of heaven so fine That all the world will be in love with night And pay no worship to the garish sun.

—William Shakespeare, *Romeo and Juliet*

The evening of Friday, December 7, 2018, started off much like most other nights. We were having our annual holiday party the following evening. Not wanting to have to clean up the kitchen for the party, we decided to order our dinner to be delivered from a local Japanese restaurant. Bob had chicken katsu and a Peroni, his favorite beer, while I enjoyed sushi and a glass (or two) of Pinot Grigio.

Our conversation focused on how we were going to fit the thirty or so guests who were coming to our party into our apartment. We had planned a catered affair. The hors d'oeuvres would be prepared right in our kitchen by two chefs from What's the Kitch, a local catering company, and passed by a server. Baby lamb chops and mini-ravioli in a sage brown butter sauce were among the appetizers we had selected for our menu. Food and a full bar of drinks would be available throughout the four-hour event. And caroling was going to be led by Ed Palermo, whose "Big Band" often plays at The Iridium in midtown Manhattan.

We went to bed early, wanting to get a good rest before our party. Bob put on soft music as he did every night. As usual, we fell asleep holding hands. But at about two o'clock in the morning, I realized that Bob was no longer in bed beside me. I figured he had gone to the bathroom, and I called out to see if he was okay.

I was usually aware whenever he got up, but that night was different. It was strangely quiet and I had not heard him get out of bed. Since he didn't answer, I decided to get up to investigate. When I found him, he had collapsed on the bathroom floor. I thought maybe he had passed out or lost his balance and fallen—at least I hoped that was what had happened.

I immediately called Victor, the building superintendent, assuming he would be able to help get Bob back on his feet, as he had done many times before. But when Victor came up to our apartment and tried to help Bob, he quickly realized something much more serious was going on. He told me to call 911, and they told Victor how to begin CPR.

The rest of the night was a chaotic blur. First, I called my daughter, who rushed over from her nearby apartment in twenty minutes or so. By then, the emergency technicians and police had arrived. The medics tried to bring Bob back as I stood there in stunned disbelief. At some point, they assured me that they could do just as much for Bob there at our apartment as they could at the hospital. I was relieved about that and glad he was home. However, after about thirty minutes of efforts, they told me that nothing more could be done.

So, they removed the wedding band I had put on Bob's finger that beautiful evening when we had finally been married. I placed it on my left hand, right next to the rings he had given me, and where it remains to this day.

The medical examiner was the last to arrive at the apartment. He asked Anna and me to leave the room so he could check Bob over. Then he told us we could come back in to say our goodbyes. And just like that, at 2:55 a.m. on Saturday, December 8, 2018, my dear husband was gone.

And I was a widow.

CHAPTER 4

FALLING INTO GRIEF

Grief can't be shared. Everyone carries it alone. His own burden in his own way.

—Anne Morrow Lindbergh

When I fully realized Bob had passed away, I experienced a wide range of emotions. I felt disbelief that he was really gone. It had been so sudden and unexpected I could barely comprehend what had happened. I was angry. Why had I been cheated out of what I had hoped for and expected? Life wasn't fair, at least not to me. I had thought I had my days planned, that Bob would be my companion, the constant in my life. That every night I would have dinner with him. I would go to sleep with him by my side. That he would love, care for, and protect me. I finally had unconditional love and it had vanished in a flash. I was alone and I had no preparation, no advance warning. I was in a fog. I was sad. I was grieving.

Grief is a natural reaction to the loss of a loved one. Grief, after all, is love with no place to go. In fact, a popular inventory of stress ranks the loss of a spouse as *the* single most stressful life event.

Recently, I had dinner with a close friend, Dr. Pauline Boss, professor emeritus in the Department of Family Social Science at the University of Minnesota. Pauline's husband passed away in 2020. Their marriage was a long and happy one. We talked a lot that evening about the idea of "closure," of finality. In her latest book, *The Myth of Closure: Ambiguous Loss in a Time of Pandemic*, she wrote that the need for closure is not found in most cultures; it is largely an American phenomenon. She believes we don't get *over* the loss of a loved one and move on (i.e., achieve closure). Rather we move *forward* and *through* grief, integrating the loss into our very being so that it becomes a part of us. The situation may have changed, but the bond with the person who has passed away continues as we learn to live with loss and grief, even ultimately finding meaning from it. As the evening with Pauline drew to a close, I asked her if she felt happy now. She told me, "Not exactly happy, but content, with occasional feelings of joy!" Perhaps that sense of contentment is something to strive for.

Grief can affect a person in many ways. It is normal to feel shock, sadness, loneliness, even anger. An initial reaction is often denial. Grief causes actual changes in the brain that can bring about these symptoms. A small number of widows experience "broken heart syndrome" where they pass away shortly after their deceased spouse.

There is no one right way to grieve or a set timetable for moving ahead. Grief is as individual as the person who is suffering. For me, grief has softened over time but it is still there, making some days sadder than others. When that happens, I acknowledge that I have what I have come to call "the sads" and remind myself that the feeling will pass.

I was traumatized when Bob passed away. It happened so suddenly it was difficult to process what had occurred. I just knew that in a split second my world had changed forever. But it took a while to grasp fully how enormous that change would be.

My last memory of my husband was seeing him being wheeled out of our apartment in a body bag. Sadly, we never got to say goodbye but I found comfort in that our last evening together was a simple, pleasant, "normal" time with just the two of us. And at least I knew I told him I loved him that day, as I did every day.

A typical reaction to grief is brain fog, or grief brain. Grief changes the brain; the symptoms of forgetfulness, trouble sleeping, and difficulty concentrating become commonplace. I don't remember much about the first few weeks after Bob had passed away. I was fortunate my daughter stayed with me for about a month. Even after she had returned to her nearby apartment, she looked in on me often. I don't know how I would have managed without her love and support.

Widowed friends experiencing brain fog have mentioned trying to turn a TV on with their phone or having a sense of aloneness when in a crowd. One friend described this as feeling "frozen in time." Another, who loved to read, told me she couldn't manage to read more than a page at a time. I have had that same problem. Yet another widow described her difficulties with simple math, like balancing her checkbook or dealing with the financial affairs of her late husband. For some widows, remembering names of familiar people or the dates of important appointments can be a challenge. Brain fog typically lasts about twelve months. For some, the duration is much briefer. For others, it may last longer. The important thing to remember is that it is a temporary condition.

Having dinner together was always a special time for Bob and me and we made a bit of a production out of it. We often cooked together or had meals delivered from nearby restaurants. We typically started our evening with drinks (Scotch or single malt for him, white wine for me) and some simple appetizers, often cheese and crackers or guacamole and chips. Then we'd either make dinner (fajitas or pasta were often on the menu) or order in (frequently Chinese food or sushi). Sometimes we had company, but most nights it was just the two of us. We did that every night. It was a tradition I counted on. But after Bob was gone, it was over.

Apparently, many widows find mealtime particularly difficult. In the four years since Bob passed away, I haven't cooked once. I try to have company a couple nights a week, although the pandemic lockdown thwarted that for about a year. Usually, I'll have something delivered from a local restaurant or my daughter will cook. And when I'm alone I still can't sit at the dining room table. Bob's sister, Candy, suggested I set a place for him where he used to sit across from me. But I can't do that. It would be too wrenching emotionally. So, if I'm alone, which is most evenings, I'll either eat standing up in the kitchen or in front of the television in the living room.

I remember my widowed mother telling me she had no appetite, that nothing appealed.

And I would tell her she should force herself. Now I understand.

BOB LOVED ITALIAN FOOD.
(Photo by the author.)

CHAPTER 5

HOW I COPED

You cannot prevent the birds of sorrow from flying over your head, but you can prevent them from building nests in your hair.

—Old Chinese Proverb

How people cope is as variable as how people grieve. In the early days and weeks after Bob passed away, sometimes all I could do was get out of bed, get dressed, and perhaps take a shower. I couldn't sleep. I didn't eat much either. But, realizing that self-care is crucial, I tried to do a bit more every day. It was tough, but looking back after six months or so, I was surprised to see how far I'd come by taking it one day at a time since those difficult early days!

I was interested in reading about what I was experiencing as a new widow. A search turned up hundreds of books about coping with grief, dealing with the challenges of widowhood, and the phenomenon of near-death experiences. Some of the most helpful of these readings are listed in the appendix of this book.

I became interested in reading books by psychic mediums about signs and visits from loved ones who had passed. These signs began for me the day after Bob passed away when my daughter and I heard some unfamiliar sounds after dinner. Then, several days later when I was having dinner with a few friends in my apartment, different sounds occurred and we all heard them. A quick check of the apartment showed nothing was amiss. So, I started to think maybe Bob was checking in.

I felt fortunate to have gotten signs so early. For some, it apparently takes longer—or may not happen at all. I have had more than two hundred signs and visits so far. In addition, since the beginning of the pandemic, exactly every six hours for over three years, I have heard a series of knocks that continue to this day. The patterns of the knocks may differ from day to day, but the timing is always exactly every six hours. My apartment lights have flickered or turned off and on, televisions have turned on spontaneously, and objects have gone missing or have been moved around. I remember finding some missing kitchen towels stuffed in a drawer in the living room. I've even actually seen Bob briefly at the foot of our bed or dashing through the living room. And once I felt him in bed behind me.

I asked Bob what it's like where he is now. He told me it's "beautiful." I wanted to know if he ate and he said he didn't need to, nor did he have a body. "It's all energy here," he said. Finally, he promised to come for me when it's my time—and then he vanished. It was all over in a few seconds, but it was very real rather than a dream. These experiences are not frightening; they have brought me comfort and reassurance that Bob is very much still with me. I'm glad I was open to them.

I have also had two life-changing readings via Zoom from psychic medium Drew Cali, who described messages from Bob that have confirmed my belief that there is an afterlife beyond what we understand. Drew conveyed information about Bob and me that could not be found online. Through Drew, Bob told me what happened the night he passed away was what was meant to happen. It was his time. He also said I was his rock, that we were meant to be together and that nothing had been left unsaid between us. These were exactly the sorts of things Bob would tell me when he was alive. He also wanted me to know he is watching over me and protecting me. I read a number of fascinating memoirs by psychic mediums such as Matt Fraser, with whom I later had a reassuring reading over the phone. These readings, and several others, were probably the most powerfully effective things I did to cope.

Reaching out to people—both new friends and old—has helped me stay connected and staved off feelings of loneliness. Like so many widows I've spoken to, I was dismayed by how many old "friends" simply disappeared. People I thought would be there for me never even checked in! I had to look outside my usual circle. I've especially appreciated those friends who would talk to me about Bob, sit with me to look at pictures of happier times, and, if they knew him, share their own memories. But simply being there, sitting quietly with me, helped, too.

One widowed friend has found companionship and understanding from a group of widows she met when their husbands were in the same hospice program. They connect every few weeks via Zoom or in person, going out to brunch or simply chatting, and now laughing. After several years, they have become family.

There are many groups on Facebook for widows. An excellent group is The Modern Widows Club. This is an international organization whose aim is to empower widows. It has travel groups, a book club, an informative newsletter, and more. I have become involved with this group by publishing some of my writings in their newsletter. Another Facebook group of very supportive and understanding people is Widows and Widowers Grief Support Group.

People in these two groups really "get" the magnitude of the loss. These and other helpful groups are listed in the appendix.

Widows whose husbands died while in hospice mention how group sessions led by trained practitioners either in person or on Zoom have helped them sort out their feelings and find support in their grief. And if the grief is overwhelming, formal therapy may help.

Anniversaries of important events such as birthdays and holidays can be especially daunting. I believe life should be celebrated and I like to acknowledge these days by being with my daughter and sometimes a few friends, enjoying a special dinner and perhaps make a toast of Prosecco in Bob's honor. On the first anniversary of his passing, I threw our annual Christmas party in his memory. My guests and I ate, drank, laughed, and sang carols. I'm sure Bob was watching with joy!

Some widows have found volunteering to be especially meaningful. One friend has started volunteering in an animal shelter where she is particularly taken with the "senior" cats. She even gave a fourteen-year-old kitty, Foxy Roxy, a forever home. Others enjoy traveling with family, friends, or even alone. One widowed friend came to New York City every year with her husband where they have a timeshare. She now does that alone, visiting friends, enjoying restaurants, and going to the opera at the Lincoln Center.

There are numerous ways to keep the memory of a loved one alive. That was an important goal for me. The Amyloidosis Foundation is a group that promotes awareness of and encourages research about this rare condition, the disease Bob had when he passed away. I have had fundraisers to support their important work. I have also established the Bob Zappa Memorial Scholarship Fund (BZMSF) in his memory with Young Performers International (YPI), a group that brings music experiences to children. This fund helps low income and learning different children participate. Each child is even given a free instrument of their choice. The BZMSF has provided tuition assistance so children in financial need can attend the YPI summer music camp. It feels very satisfying to make a difference in these young lives.

THE BROCHURE FOR THE BOB ZAPPA
MEMORIAL SCHOLARSHIP FUND.

CHAPTER 6

HOW WRITING EASED MY PAIN

I can shake off everything if I write; my sorrows disappear, my courage is reborn.

—Anne Frank

Almost immediately after Bob passed away, I started to write. I had to find a way to ease the pain of his passing and thought writing a memoir or keeping a journal might help. I've always enjoyed writing. I'd already written a few college textbooks. I was even editor of my high school yearbook. Writing to ease my pain was different, but it made sense to me. I hoped that reflecting on my loss would be cathartic, allowing me to find meaning in my experience. And eventually peace.

A few months after Bob died, I started to write about the trauma. My writing came naturally and easily. It felt good to get it out! Sometimes I'd "write" in my head before putting my pen to paper—or in my case, fingers to iPad.

I organized my thoughts in chapters rather than as a journal. I didn't work from an outline. I didn't need one. The chapters flowed easily. At times, I felt I was channeling Bob. On a good day, I'd often draft a couple chapters. And I wrote every day. I needed to.

I never intended to publish my musings. I wanted to preserve my memories before they inevitably started to fade. And I wanted to share the story of Bob and me with my daughter, Anna, and a few friends. I hoped I'd find comfort in collecting my memories so I could go back to them at any time. When I wrote, I let the words simply flow, allowing me to express and confront many powerful emotions without worrying about grammar or punctuation. Writing increased my sense of well-being and decreased my anxiety and depression.

Then, one day in August 2020, I was scrolling through my Facebook feed. Emily Barrosse, who had been an editor-in-chief at McGraw Hill, had posted that she just founded Bold Story Press. A pretty bold move in the middle of a pandemic! And I admired that. She said she was looking for manuscripts by women to evaluate for publication; she was familiar with my textbooks. I replied to her post telling her I had a manuscript. It was a story of two soulmates, Bob and Diane, who fell in love in 1986, finally got together in 2013, and married in 2015. And then, in 2018, Bob passed away.

She was intrigued. We had a lengthy phone call the next day in which I "pitched" my story. She asked me to send whatever I had written. I explained I wrote on my iPad using the Evernote app. Even though it might be unorthodox, she said I should send it on. So, I sent her a table of contents and three chapters. After a few weeks, she told me Bold Story Press wanted to publish my memoir. I signed a contract and in July 2021, *The Married Widow: My Journey with Bob Zappa,* was published. It was the first book published by Bold Story Press.

Before publishing *The Married Widow*, I had begun my "Dear Bobby" letters, a collection of letters to Bob to tell him about my life and feelings. I enjoyed the challenge of determining what I wanted to tell him. I have compiled some of my favorite letters in Part Two of this book. And Part Three includes quotes by famous individuals that can serve as writing prompts, or may simply serve as ideas for thought and reflection.

THE COVER OF THE AUTHOR'S MEMOIR.

PART TWO

THE
DEAR BOBBY
LETTERS

WRITING TO BOB

After Bob died, I began to write him letters, something I still do to this day. In my "Dear Bobby" letters, I share with him memories of things we enjoyed together and explain how I'm doing. Writing to him allows our relationship to continue. It helps keep him near and keeps our love alive. There is no set time or place when the inspiration for a letter would come to me. Often, it was early in the morning while still in bed. Or it could come while I was sipping a cup of coffee or enjoying a glass of wine. It is my way of talking with him at any time or in any place.

The following is a selection of those letters.

July 28, 2019

Dear Bobby,

So, I think this will be my new project. Writing to you as the spirit (so to speak) moves me. I really miss being with you, having dinner, cooking, joking around, the cocktail hour. The little things that make up a life together. I miss turning down the sheets with you before we go out. I miss you turning on the music before we would go to sleep. I haven't been able to do that since you passed away. I miss you asking me if I'm cold and then turning your back to me to warm me up. I miss checking if that solitary hair had grown back on your nose.

I simply miss you.

Love,

Diane

August 10, 2019

Dear Bobby,

It's our cocktail hour and I'm sitting in the living room across from your chair. You're not there, but every night, around 6:15, I begin our usual tradition by grabbing a glass of white wine and sitting in my chair. I raise a toast to you, and tell you that I love and miss you. Then I turn on the corner table lamp in case you want to send me a hello by flicking it. I love when you do that. Some nights there is, at best, a tiny little flicker. But when you have something more urgent to tell me, you flicker and I respond. Sometimes it goes on for a few minutes, reminding me that you are here. But most nights, nothing happens any more. I'd love more flickering because it comforts me. Can you help me?

Love,

Diane

August 15, 2019

Dear Bobby,

I woke up early this morning and put the coffee on. I always set it up the night before so I can start it without a fuss. I don't know why I didn't think of doing that when you were here.

I remember how you would bring me coffee in bed every day, right until the end. You placed a full cup on the seat of your walker and rolled it into our bedroom. When I needed a refill, I would holler your name and you'd bring me a second cup. Or a third. You struggled to get the coffee from the walker to the bedside table; your fingers didn't want to let go of the cup. But you did it. You never gave up. And I admired that so much.

I remember once, shortly before you passed away, you brought me my coffee and asked if I ever regretted marrying you.

Not for a second. Not even once.

Love,

Diane

August 19, 2019

Dear Bobby,

I've been thinking about how we lost touch with each other before we married, and I hadn't heard from you for seven long years. Then you wrote to tell me your wife had passed, and I couldn't believe it!

But I was at a low point. I couldn't walk; my hips were so bad that I needed a walker to get around. I wanted so badly to see you, but I was afraid if you saw me with my walker, you would run the other way.

We talked and talked on the phone, but it took me many weeks to get up the courage to tell you what a mess I was. Still, you didn't let that stop you. The first weekend we spent together was magic. I loved hearing—many weeks later—what you felt when you saw me. You said I looked at you with such hope. And you thought, "This is the woman I love and I'm going to make it better." And that's exactly what you did.

Love,

Diane

September 5, 2019

Dear Bobby,

This morning I am thinking again about how you contacted me after years of silence, after your wife had died. Your letter arrived in August 2013; a friend brought it up to me along with a stack of bills, catalogs, and junk. It was in a plain white envelope with my name and address typed out. There was no return address. It was at the bottom of the pile and because it looked like junk mail, I almost didn't open it. But when I did, I murmured, "It's from Bob." I wrote back right away, telling you, "I still love you and always will. I am alone."

I wonder if you would have tried to contact me again if I hadn't replied. You had reassured me that you would have. But how? I'm so glad you wrote to me. By taking that chance, you started us on a path where we both, finally, found unconditional love.

I will love you forever.

Love,

Diane

September 13, 2019

Dear Bobby,

I was thinking about nicknames when I woke up this morning. You only had two for me. The first was Mimsie, which you explained was from the play *Plaza Suite*. You called me that when you wanted me to calm down about something—as in, "Cool it, Mimsie!" Your other nickname for me was Barney because I was like a barnacle, always attached to your right arm! I had several nicknames for you. For a brief while you were Borden, Mimsie's counterpart. I also called you Chuck (short for Charles) and Gabby (after Gabby Hayes when you needed a shave). But the name that really stuck was Goat. You actually named yourself that after you came home from surgery and couldn't shower for two weeks! I still think of you as Goat; not after an aroma, but because it just seemed to fit. To me you'll always be the Greatest of All Time!

Love,

Diane

September 20, 2019

Dear Bobby,

How I loved our cocktail hours! That was our special time amid many special times. One tradition that meant so much to me was right at the beginning. We'd go into the kitchen. I'd be scurrying around getting drinks and snacks together. And every night you would stand there with your back to the counter, look at me so lovingly, and motion for me to come to you. Then you'd take me in your arms and say, "Never gonna let you go." And I'd sigh and tell you those words were magical to me. *Are* magical to me. And they always will be.

Love,
Diane

September 26, 2019

Dear Bobby,

It's Thursday, the day Fresh Direct puts new items on sale. On Thursday when you were here, I'd pour over the week's offerings. "Want muffins? They're on sale," I'd say. "Yes, please." "Corn or blueberry?" "Corn." "They have jumbo blueberries this week—$7 for one container, $12 for two." "Two." "Do we need beer? Peroni, right?"

I ordered Shepherd's pie, Marie Callender's chicken pot pie, tater tots, corn on the cob, artichokes, English muffins, cinnamon raisin bread, peanut butter, avocados. I always wanted to be sure we had everything you loved.

Now, one of the hardest things I do is order from Fresh Direct. When I see your favorites, all gathered in one place, it brings back one of those precious memories that are meaningful only to you and me. I really don't cook any more. I only use Fresh Direct for bulky items: water, wine, flowers, and a few snacks. Most nights, I get a meal delivery from Seamless, like Mac and cheese. Burgers. Dumplings. Whatever.

Every so often, Anna cooks. And we sit in the dining room and talk and talk. She has claimed your chair. I'm sure you would approve.

Love,

Diane

October 10, 2019
Dear Bobby,

I remember our talks about "leaving the planet." The very idea upset me, and I asked you not to put it that way. But I'm pretty sure neither one of us thought that day was right around the corner.

You told me you would not have lasted as long as you did if I had not been with you, and that if I passed away first, you would have to leave our home because you couldn't imagine being here without me. You thought your days would be numbered if I weren't around. We always got so much energy from each other that that may have been the case. As for me, I told you that I would want to stay in this apartment because it's where so many of our memories took place. It's where we lived. And where you died. I will never leave this sacred place.

Love,
Diane

October 12, 2019

Dear Bobby,

You didn't believe in an afterlife. "This is it," you would say. That was one of the very few things we disagreed on. I firmly believed in an afterlife, of our spirits continuing on after death.

I was so happy when you sent signs to me so quickly after you passed away. There aren't as many now, but I am grateful for those you still send. They are very comforting to me. I bet you are enjoying your newfound "abilities." I wonder: what do you think about an afterlife now?

Love,

Diane

October 15, 2019

Dear Bobby,

Before we were reunited in 2013, I noticed that you had checked out my profile on LinkedIn. So, having had a glass or two of vino, I sent you a request to connect. When I got up the next morning, I regretted having done that. I figured that after our very difficult breakup seven years earlier, I was the last person you wanted to hear from. I was going to try to cancel my request, but by then you had already accepted it. Then you wrote to me and I responded. The rest is history.

Love,

Diane

May 21, 2021
Dear Bobby,

It's been a long time since I've written, and I have missed doing that, and regret it. Things here on planet Earth have been decidedly strange, though, as the Coronavirus (COVID-19) has threatened New York, the country, and eventually the entire world. Do you know about that?

New York was completely locked down. Everyone wore masks and tried to stay ten feet apart (what was called "social distancing") and washed their hands constantly. Hospitals were overflowing. Hospital tents were set up in Central Park. Everyone stayed home and avoided socializing. Even Anna couldn't visit me, so we communicated using FaceTime. It was a scary time as thousands of victims died in New York City alone.

But like cicadas emerging out of the underground, New Yorkers are beginning to emerge from their apartments, and starting to be out and about. New York City is returning to "normal," thanks to a new Coronavirus vaccine.

Isolation has been so hard. I've often thought that we would have done just fine together, because we were home together for three years before the lockdown. These days, I still hear the sounds you make to communicate with me from beyond every six hours—the clicks and knocks—that tell me you are right here watching over me. And that has made all the difference.

Love,

Diane

May 22, 2021

Dear Bobby,

One of the things I remember most fondly is when we'd wake up together every morning, you right next to me. Before going to the kitchen to make your breakfast and my coffee, you'd hold me in your arms, brush my hair away from my face, and kiss me on the forehead. Then you'd murmur "Good morning, Mrs. Z." It's such a precious memory. And I miss it.

Love,

Diane

May 30, 2021

Dear Bobby,

I've had a few readings from psychic mediums. One of them told me you were concerned that I spend so much time by myself. Here's what's helped. First, reaching out to people. Some "friends" completely vanished (I've heard that's common but you would be shocked about those who did that), but many more emerged. Talking with them, sharing memories of you, just saying your name, has made a big difference.

I also joined several grief support groups on Facebook and I made a dear friend through one of those groups. Lana's husband, Paul, passed on December 15, 2018—exactly one week after you. We provide each other a lot of mutual support and now some laughs, as well. We even message each other reminders when a favorite show (like *Shark Tank*) or a favorite movie (like *Pretty Woman* or *Legally Blonde*) is airing.

Love,
Diane

May 31, 2021

Dear Bobby,

Your sister has been amazing. As you know, Candy welcomed me into your family right after our wedding. And after you passed in December 2018, she was there with constant love, support, encouragement, and an unwavering belief that you had simply transitioned!

Her husband, Nolan Porter, passed away in February, just three months ago. So, sadly, we have shared the journey of coping with irreversible loss and the grief involved. I hope I can support and help her as much as she has been there for me. I will certainly try.

Love,

Diane

June 5, 2021
Dear Bobby,

In order to keep my memories alive, I started making lists. I didn't want to forget anything. I began by listing things you liked to eat—shrimp tacos, chicken fajitas, my mom's pasta sauce, sausage and peppers, linguine with oil, garlic, anchovies, and capers. I loved cooking for you and enjoyed doing that together. I wonder which you liked best.

I introduced you to soft shell crabs. I'd prepare them with capers in a lemon butter sauce with a dash of white wine. A quick sauté, and they were delicious. I can see you now, sitting across the dining room table, enjoying your new discovery.

These days, I don't cook. I order in most nights and eat standing in the kitchen, unless I have company. Usually, though, I go to the spot by the kitchen counter where every night you would hold me and tell me you'd never let me go. I'm most comfortable there.

I haven't had one meal sitting alone at our table. Maybe someday? Your sister suggested I set a place at the table for you. But I'm not sure I could do that, even two and a half years later.

Love,
Diane

June 24, 2021

Dear Bobby,

One of the first things I did after you passed was start reading everything I could find about the afterlife. There was plenty to choose from. I read books by psychic mediums like Matt Fraser and James Van Praagh, books about near-death experiences, and books on how to communicate with loved ones on the other side. I read enough to be awarded a PhD in Afterlife Studies, should one exist.

Early on, the books I found most helpful were those describing afterlife signs and visits. Immediately after you were gone, I realized that you were sending me a lot of different signs. Lights would turn off and on, televisions would turn on by themselves, objects would disappear or be moved, and I've found coins on the floor a few times. Once, a decorative straw chicken "flew" off the top shelf of a bookcase and landed on the floor halfway across the office. One morning shortly after you passed away, the fragrance of the perfume you gave me, Chance by L'Oréal, infused our bedroom for a few hours. Later, when I looked at the bottle, the level of the perfume had been reduced by half!

As of today, I've had over two hundred signs. You are a very active spirit indeed.

Love,

Diane

June 27, 2021

Dear Bobby,

It's been just over two and a half years since you passed away. Every day I ask why. Sometimes I scream it out loud in the shower. Sometimes I whisper it as the tears roll down my cheeks. But the question is always the same: "Why?"

Love,

Diane

May 31, 2022
Dear Bobby,

On Sunday, June 8, 2019, six months after you passed away, I had a gathering at our place to celebrate your life. I'm pretty sure you know that already. In fact, I think you were there.

Dweezil and Megan drove up from Philly; Pauline flew in from Minneapolis; Denny and Janet came all the way from Atlanta; Al, Duncan, and Ken from the gun club drove in from Jersey. And a lot of our friends who live nearby joined us.

Many people reminisced about how they knew you. Denny talked about how you had hung out together since 1955, when you met in Lancaster, CA. Anna shared how much she cared about you. Nick mentioned how he made linguine with cockles for dinner one evening. And your nephew, Dweezil, gave an emotional tribute that brought tears to my eyes.

The evening started off mysteriously. As the event got under way, I discovered all three of my rings had vanished from my left hand. I knew I'd been wearing them fifteen minutes before the party started at six o'clock. But sometime between 5:45 and 6:10 when Megan said she noticed I wasn't wearing my rings, they disappeared, not to be found until six months later, all nestled together in the bottom of the ice bin in the freezer. The amazing thing is I never felt them being taken off! I hope someday when we're together again you will tell me how you did that.

Because I'm sure it was you!

Love,

Diane

July 15, 2022
Dear Bobby,

I try to keep up on the research findings about amyloidosis. There is a group I follow called Amyloidosis Foundation that reports current progress in the treatment of the disease. I get their newsletter but, frankly, it can be hard to read. Since you passed away there has been a lot of progress. I'm glad about that. But I ask myself, why couldn't that information have been available for your treatment? And then I remember psychic medium Drew Cali told me that you said your time had simply come. And that helps.

Love,
Diane

August 29, 2022

Dear Bobby,

Since you left, I've become aware of the terminology about death. People don't "die" any more. They pass away or transition! And when that happens, you are awarded your "angel wings." Even pets don't die, but go to the Rainbow Bridge. The anniversary of the date of your transition is your "angelversary." And when I google "angelversary," all sorts of suggestions come up about how to celebrate that special date.

Actually, Anna and I always celebrate the important days: your birthday, our anniversary, and the anniversary of the day you passed. We make a special dinner that we often share with a few friends; we reminisce and toast your memory. No tears now, just happy memories.

Love,

Diane

September 1, 2022

Dear Bobby,

I've had several remarkable readings from psychic mediums. You must know, since you were there. You sent me so many loving messages. It was almost like you were here, in our home, telling me the things you would say when you were alive. Psychic medium Matt Fraser told me he saw you holding a book. I told him about the textbooks I'd already written, but he said no, a new book. The next month, I was scrolling through Facebook and saw that Emily Barrosse (do you remember her from when you were both at McGraw Hill?) had just started Bold Story Press and was looking for manuscripts by women to evaluate. I told her I'd written about 90 percent of a manuscript about us. She asked me to send what I'd written. She loved it, gave me a contract, and in July 2021, *The Married Widow: My Journey with Bob Zappa,* was published.

I must say, it has been an interesting journey indeed.

Love,

Diane

October 29, 2022

Dear Bobby,

Ever since you passed away, I had been trying to figure out what to do with your clothing. I couldn't bear to sort through it. It was easier emotionally just to keep it here, in the closet where you left it.

But then one day in September 2021, Hurricane Ida caused widespread damage, flooding, and death in New York City. Sadly, one of the porters in our building lost everything. I packed up your clothes and gave him eight large bags of shirts, sweats, sweaters, even underwear and socks. He kept what he could use and gave what was left to his neighbors in need. This was the perfect thing to do.

However, I did keep a few things that reminded me of you: the tuxedo you wore to our wedding, a couple suits and ties, a nice dress shirt, some plaid pants you'd lounge around in, and quite a few T-shirts. I couldn't part with everything.

So now, every so often, I open your closet and see what remains of your clothes. Sometimes I'll touch one or two things and bury my head in them, perhaps hoping to find a little of your scent.

And then I close the door.

And weep.

Love,
Diane

December 15, 2022

Dear Bobby,

I'm sitting in our living room across from your chair. The six o'clock news is on, and I'm having a glass of Pinot Grigio. Every night, I toast to you. Your chair is empty now, but our having drinks together every evening is still a tradition I honor.

But wait. Is that chair really empty? I'm not so sure any more.

Psychic medium Patty MacGillivray and I have become friends. I recently had a text from her. She said she had a message for me from you: you told her that every night you "sit" in your chair across from me and enjoy my company. You even gave Patty an accurate description of that chair: old, velvet seat, placed across from where I sit.

Are you really there in spirit? I hope so.

As we Italians say, "*Cin. Cin.*"

Love,

Diane

February 4, 2023

Dear Bobby,

It has been a really strange winter here. It took until February 1 to have any measurable snow in the city, ending a three hundred twenty-eight day stretch of snowless days, breaking a fifty-year record! And what finally came down melted so fast it was easy to miss.

The temperature has been strange, too. It's freezing today. Even our apartment is cold. But starting tomorrow, a stretch of weather in the fifties is predicted. Right now, it's five degrees outside. The wind chill factor is minus eleven. But there have been a few days this winter when it's been warm enough to turn the A/C on!

Is this the climate change we hear so much about?

Love,

Diane

March 4, 2023

Dear Bobby,

What was it like to die? I guess it was quick and I hope painless, as you left our bed in the middle of the night and only ten minutes later, I found that you had collapsed on the bathroom floor.

Did you see the EMTs trying to breathe life into you? Did you see me standing in stunned silence or Anna in tears? Did you "know" when Anna brought me over to your lifeless body and gave me your hand so I could hold it one last time?

Was there a tunnel and a white light? Did your brother Frank come to be with you as you transitioned from this world to the next? Who else was waiting to welcome you?

I wonder, too, what it will be like for me. Will you be the one to bring me home?

Love,

Diane

PART THREE

START YOUR WRITING JOURNEY

LET THE WORDS FLOW

Journaling is a powerful way to deal with grief. Writing about an experience, whether using pen and paper, a computer, or an iPad like I did, gives writers an opportunity to reflect on and confront their thoughts and feelings. Writing about feelings is cathartic. By writing about a painful experience, such as the death of a beloved spouse, stress should be lessened. I found simply writing about Bob's passing helped me acknowledge my feelings and deal with them, and this eased my pain. The more I wrote, the more relief I felt.

There is no one "right" way to journal, just as there is no one "right" way to grieve or to cope with grief. But it's most beneficial if journaling is done regularly. Don't worry about style or grammar. Just let the words flow.

I have chosen a selection of quotes to reflect on and write about. The quotes at the beginning of each chapter in Part One can be used the same way.

People, such as widows who have suffered a loss, might use these prompts as a way to start thinking about their loss and to start their writing. But even people who haven't had that painful experience can benefit from reflecting on these ideas.

Find some that are appealing, and start writing!

***

Love is composed of a single soul inhabiting two bodies.

—ARISTOTLE, ancient Greek philosopher

Death ends a life, not a relationship.

—MITCH ALBOM, from *Tuesdays with Morrie*

Grief is the price we pay for love.

—QUEEN ELIZABETH II, in her message to those who lost loved ones in the 9/11 terrorist attacks in New York City

An invisible thread connects those who are destined to meet, regardless of time, space, and circumstance. The thread may stretch or tangle, but it will never break.

—Old Chinese proverb

Pain passes but the beauty remains.

—PIERRE-AUGUSTE RENOIR, impressionist painter

There is no greater agony than bearing an untold story inside you.

—MAYA ANGELOU, from *I Know Why the Caged Bird Sings*

Preserve your memories, keep them well, what you forget you can never retell.

—LOUISA MAY ALCOTT, American author best known for *Little Women*

Grief changes shape, but it never ends.

—KEANU REEVES, Canadian actor, as told to *Parade Magazine*

In the midst of winter, I found there was, within me, an invincible summer.

—ALBERT CAMUS, French-Algerian philosopher and author

How lucky I am to have something that makes saying goodbye so hard.

—A.A. MILNE, from *The Complete Tales of Winnie-the-Pooh*

Grief makes one hour ten.

—WILLIAM SHAKESPEARE, from *Richard II*

You gain strength, courage, and confidence by every experience in which you really stop to look fear in the face.

—**ELEANOR ROOSEVELT, from** *You Learn by Living: Eleven Keys for a More Fulfilling Life*

Life has been painfully split into a "before" and "after"

My heart won't let me forget.

—**LIZ NEWMAN, from** *I Look to the Mourning Sky: A Book of Poems and Writing Prompts for the Grieving Heart*

Tis better to have loved and lost than never to have loved at all.

—**ALFRED, LORD TENNYSON, from the elegiac poem "In Memoriam A.H.H."**

We must be willing to let go of the life we had planned so as to have the life that is waiting for us.

—**JOSEPH CAMPBELL, American author**

Tears are words that need to be written.

—**PAULO COELHO, Brazilian lyricist and author**

Grief carves a place in the heart and sits there forever. But when focused, it can be a powerful motivator. Sadness becomes resolve and pain becomes action.

—From the British fantasy television series, A Discovery of Witches

APPENDIX

RESOURCES FOR THOSE WHO ARE GRIEVING

People are usually unprepared for widowhood. I know I was. I didn't expect it, and didn't have a clue about how to deal with it. It was a long journey, but I've come through it as a survivor. I found the "invincible summer" Albert Camus described. And I'm proud of that.

I was amazed to read some statistics. There are more than 13.7 million widowed people in the United States, and 11.8 million of them are women. About 2,800 women are joining "the club nobody wants to belong to" every day. The average age of becoming a widow in the U.S. is an astonishing fifty-nine, making becoming a widow a normative event of midlife, rather than old age.

The following are a few resources that helped me understand Bob's death and helped me cope with my grief. I hope at least some of these may prove to be helpful to you, too.

BOOKS ABOUT DEATH AND GRIEF

I have read these books and highly recommend them. These are available as either physical books or eBooks. This selection includes both classic and more contemporary offerings.

- *Modern Loss: Candid Conversations About Grief. Beginners Welcome.* Rebecca Soffer and Gabrielle Bircher (2018)

- *The Other Side of Sadness: What the New Science of Bereavement Tells Us About Life After Loss.* George A. Bonanno (2019)

- *The Myth of Closure: Ambiguous Loss in a Time of Pandemic and Change.* Pauline Boss (2021)

- *Bearing the Unbearable: Love, Loss, and the Heartbreaking Path of Grief.* Dr. Joanne Cacciatore (2017)

- *It's Ok That You're Not Ok: Meeting Grief and Loss in a Culture that Doesn't Understand.* Megan Devine (2017)

- *The Year of Magical Thinking.* Joan Didion (2007)

- *Being Mortal: Illness, Medicine, and What Matters in the End.* Atul Gawande (2014)

- *Healing After Loss: Daily Meditations for Working Through Grief.* Martha Whitmore Hickman (1994)

- *When Breath Becomes Air.* Paul Kalanithi (2016)

- *Finding Meaning: The Sixth Stage of Grief.* David Kessler (2019)

- *Embracing Life After Loss: A Gentle Guide for Growing through Grief.* Allen Klein (2019)

- *On Death and Dying: What the Dying Have to Teach Doctors, Nurses, Clergy, and Their Own Families.* Elisabeth Kübler-Ross (Originally published in 1969; commemorative edition published in 2011)

- *On Grief and Grieving: Finding the Meaning of Grief Through the Five Stages of Loss.* Elisabeth Kübler-Ross and David Kessler (2005)

- A *Grief Observed.* C.S. Lewis (Originally published in 1961, reissued in 2009)

- *How We Die: Reflections on Life's Final Chapter.* Sherwin B. Nuland (2014)

- *A Widow's Story: A Memoir.* Joyce Carol Oates (2011)

- *My Husband is Not a Rainbow: The Brutally Awful, Hilarious Truth about Life, Love, Grief, and Loss.* Kelley Lynn Shepherd (2018)

BOOKS ABOUT THE AFTERLIFE

These books opened my eyes and my thoughts to the possibility that there is life beyond what we understand here on earth. They helped me make sense of my personal experiences.

- *Proof of Heaven: A Neurosurgeon's Journey into the Afterlife.* Eben Alexander, MD (2012)

- *Hello from Heaven: A New Field of Research-After-Death Communication Confirms that Life and Love are Eternal.* Bill Guggenheim and Judy Guggenheim (1995)

- *The Afterlife of Billy Fingers: How My Bad-Boy Brother Proved to Me There's Life After Death.* Annie Kagan (2013)

- *Life After Life: The Bestselling Original Investigation that Revealed "Near Death Experiences."* Raymond Moody (Originally published in 1976, reissued in 2015)

- *Reflections on Life After Life.* Raymond Moody (2011)

- *The Light Beyond: Explorations into the Afterlife.* Raymond Moody (2016)

- *Answers about the Afterlife: A Private Investigator's 15-Year Research Unlocks the Mysteries of Life after Death.* Bob Olson (2014)

- *Signs from the Afterlife: Identifying Gifts from the Other Side.* Lyn Ragan (2014)

BOOKS BY PSYCHIC MEDIUMS

This is a fascinating collection in which reputable psychic mediums describe their experiences. I had an amazing forty-five-minute phone reading with one of them, Matt Fraser. It took two years to book an appointment, but it was worth the wait.

- *I'm Still with You: Communicate, Heal, and Evolve with Your Loved One on the Other Side.* Sherrie Dillard (2020)

- *We Never Die: Secrets of the Afterlife.* Matt Fraser (2022)

- *When Heaven Calls: Life Lessons from America's Top Psychic Medium.* Matt Fraser (2020)

- *Signs: The Secret Language of the Universe.* Laura Lynne Jackson (2019)

- *Never Argue with a Dead Person: True and Unbelievable Stories from the Other Side.* Thomas John (2015)

- *Everything You Wanted to Know About the Afterlife but Were Afraid to Ask.* Hollister Rand (2020)

- *Talking to Heaven: A Medium's Message of Life After Death.* James Van Praagh (1999)

FILMS WITH AFTERLIFE THEMES

The afterlife has been an important area for exploration in film. This selection includes both classic and more contemporary offerings. Choose a few that sound interesting to you or revisit some you may have enjoyed in the past. Although no two are alike, they are all thought-provoking.

- *After Life.* A three-season Netflix series released in 2019, 2020, and 2022, starring Ricky Gervais.

- *A Guy Named Joe.* When World War II pilot, Pete Sandidge, dies in an aerial attack after ordering the crew to safety, he meets a legendary dead pilot who assigns Pete to return to Earth as a guardian angel for a new pilot named Ted Randall. A 1943 film starring Spencer Tracy, Van Johnson, and Irene Dunne.

- *Always.* A 1989 remake of *A Guy Named Joe* starring Richard Dreyfuss, John Goodman, and Holly Hunter.

- *Carousel.* The classic 1956 musical stars Gordon MacRae and Shirley Jones. A carousel barker is granted one day to return to Earth to make amends to his widow and their child.

- *Defending Your Life.* A 1991 film about a man who finds himself on trial to determine whether he'll be reincarnated on Earth. Starring Albert Brooks, Meryl Streep, and Rip Torn.

- *Ghost.* A 1990 movie starring Patrick Swayze, Demi Moore, and Whoopi Goldberg. The ghost of a young man who is murdered remains on Earth to protect his beloved from danger. Whoopi Goldberg won an Academy Award for her role as a reluctant psychic.

- *Heaven Is for Real.* After their young son, Colton (Connor Corum), undergoes emergency surgery, his parents are thrilled at the child's amazing recovery. However, they are unprepared when Colton says that he went to heaven and back. Based on a true story. Stars Greg Kinnear and was released in 2014. Adapted from the 2011 book *Heaven is for Real: A Little Boy's Astounding Story of His Trip to Heaven and Back* by Todd Burpo.

- *Hereafter.* A 2010 film starring Matt Damon. Three people set out on a spiritual journey after death touches their lives in different ways. Directed by Clint Eastwood.

- *It's a Wonderful Life.* The 1946 film starring James Stewart as George Bailey, a man who has given up his personal dreams in order to help others. His thoughts of suicide bring about the intervention of his guardian angel, Clarence Odbody, who shows George all the lives he touched and what the world would be like if he did not exist. A Christmas classic.

- *Life After Life*. An award-winning 1992 documentary that compiles over 2,000 cases of people who have had near death experiences. Based on the work of Dr. Raymond Moody, a pioneer in this area.

- *P.S. I Love You*. A 2007 release starring Gerard Butler and Hillary Swank. When Gerry is dying, he writes letters to his wife. Beginning on her thirtieth birthday, she receives the first in the series, written to ease her grief and encourage her to move forward to a new life.

- *The Ghost and Mrs. Muir*. The 1947 classic film starring Rex Harrison and Gene Tierney. A widow rents a cottage and develops an emotional relationship with its resident ghost.

- *The Sixth Sense*. A 1999 American film written and directed by M. Night Shyamalan. Starring Bruce Willis as a child psychologist whose patient claims he can see and talk to the dead.

- *Truly, Madly, Deeply*. A 1990 British fantasy starring Juliet Stevenson, Alan Rickman, Bill Paterson, and Michael

Maloney. A woman struggles to cope with the death of her lover only to find that his ghost moves back into her flat.

- *Wings of Desire.* 1987 romantic German fantasy by Wim Wenders. The story of an angel who tires of his heavenly life and desires a physical life when he falls in love with a mortal. Inspired the 1998 American movie *City of Angels* starring Meg Ryan and Nicholas Cage.

SUPPORT GROUPS

There are many support groups both online and on Facebook that offer support for people who are grieving. These are some of the best that I found.

ONLINE SUPPORT GROUPS

These groups all have websites that have lots of information online.

- Camp Widow (campwidow.org)

- Grief Share (griefshare.org)

- Modern Widows Club (modernwidowsclub.org)

- National Widower's Organization (nationalwidowers.org)

- Soaring Spirits International (soaringspirits.org)

- W Connection (widowsconnection.org)

FACEBOOK GROUPS

Facebook has many groups for widows. I have joined these and found members to be compassionate and supportive. Only a few of these accept widowers. Some of the most poignant comments are from the widowers; all participants truly grasp the immensity of their loss.

- For Widows Only (Women)

- Hope for Widows Foundation

- Modern Widows Club

- Wacky Widows

- Widow and Widowers Grief Support Group

- Widow and Widowers—Healing, Support, and Education

For those who are curious about the afterlife, these Facebook groups are interesting and informative.

- Afterlife Research and Education Discussion

- Proof of Life After Death

- Signs from our Loved Ones

- Signs from the Afterlife

- The Afterlife

The following Facebook pages contain many comforting and inspirational quotes and poems for those who are struggling.

- Daily Grief Quote

- Grief Speaks

- Liz Newman (Poems)

ACKNOWLEDGMENTS

'd like to thank the following people who encouraged me as I wrote this book, helping to make it the best possible memoir. First and foremost, heartfelt thanks to my daughter Anna V. Finlay. Her unwavering love and support helped bring my dream to write this book to fruition. A special shout out to my sister-in-law, Candy Zappa, who has been there for me as I coped with the loss of her brother Bob.

I am also indebted to the following people who read and critiqued drafts of the manuscript: Vera Armstrong, Ephraim Frankel, Marion Hook, Janet Houts, Jane Moody, Susan Nichols, Susan Palermo, Scott Parker, Leela Pratt, Lana Rudner, and Jennifer Seitzer. Thanks also to editor Karen Gulliver for her meticulous attention to detail, to Sue Balcer for her beautiful cover and interior design, to production manager Julianna Scott Fein and, of course, to Emily Barrosse for making this book a reality.

Diane Papalia Zappa
New York, New York

ABOUT THE AUTHOR

Diane Papalia Zappa graduated from Vassar College in 1968, and earned an MS and PhD from West Virginia University in 1970 and 1971, respectively. While a professor at the University of Wisconsin-Madison, she and Sally Wendkos Olds co-authored two textbooks, *A Child's World* (now in its thirteenth edition) and *Human Development* (now in its fifteenth edition).

Diane met Frank Zappa's younger brother, Bob, when he was the marketing manager for one of her textbooks. They married in 2015. Her memoir, *The Married Widow: My Journey with Bob Zappa*, tells the story of their relationship.

When not writing letters to her husband, Diane enjoys reading fiction, visiting with her daughter and friends, playing Wordle, and collecting blown-glass pumpkins. Occasionally, she will throw a grand holiday party in her apartment. She lives in New York City.